The [R]evolutionary Mindset

Transform the way you Think...Act...Live!

D1417728

The [R]evolutionary Mindset
Copyright: Fred Posimo
Front Cover/ Info-Graphic designs by Harris Yampolsky
Back Cover Photos by Jess Sariego

Contents

Acknowledgments

I want to start off by saying, nothing in this book comes from my own knowledge, it is merely a collective adaptation of those who have laid the path before me. Much comes from other books I have read. There are so many people I would like to acknowledge but words are a poor medium to articulate my feelings, however I shall try my best. Mom and Dad for your consistency, passion, love, and for always believing in me. Extreme Karate and Fitness for being my second home for the past decade and a half, for nurturing me, and forging me into who I am today. My friends, family, and all those who have brought meaning to my life. For all those who educate and inspire, you are the stars, which glimmer in the night, let more like you ascend to the skies.

Preframing...

There are three stages to any journey, the starting point, the commute, and the destination. Take a good hard look at yourself currently; this is your starting point. By the conclusion of this book your self-perception should become positively altered. As we begin traveling towards a re-invigorated future, remember to enjoy the journey. The commute is the longer endeavor; don't become so fixated on the destination that you miss all the beauty of your travels. I am not saying not to have a plan, but rather to delight in the process of attaining it. This book is not about an end result it is a transition from whom you are today into whom you have always wanted to be, lets dive in!

Of all the pursuits throughout my life one of the most impactful for nearly 15 years has been Martial Arts. Throughout these pages it will be alluded to, with many of its philosophies intertwined. I intended to open speaking about this art because in it we can find a plethora of symbolism, such as bowing. Bowing is foremost a representation of respect to others and self. However it also symbolizes having an *Empty Mind.* Legend states we are holding a teacup, which is then poured out upon bowing. This teacup represents our mind being emptied, put differently preparing to be filled. Presently this is *your* task. Before embarking on this life-fulfilling voyage, empty your mind. A seemingly insurmountable mission lay before you if proper preparation is not executed. Let your mind go, part with all pre-conceived notions temporarily and expose your mind, body, and spirit to new opportunities. My only request is that you do not simply read this book, but rather explore it, engage in it, and most importantly implement it. Approached proactively this read could be influential on your future life. Take a minute, sit calmly and "let go." Allow your mind to be at peace. Now, if you are properly prepared lets begin this quest.

Introduction

The [R]evolutionary Mindset... I know what you're thinking, "What the heck does that mean?" (And why are there ridiculous brackets around the "R," does this author have spelling issues?) I can assure you this is not the case, the brackets are intentional, we'll cover that in a minute. For now let's examine the first word "Revolutionary." According to *Webster's*, revolutionary means: "Causing or relating to a great or complete change." Lets break it down, the first word "Causing." Cause is a powerful word; it contains a deep, well-rooted connotation. Often we see changes in effects, not causes. Effects are offsets of causes. When we change causes, however, this produces deeper, more permanent solutions. As we begin to launch a revolution we alter our cause, not our effects. For some of us, to get from where we are to where we want to go it requires a revolution.

In order to make this more graspable let's consider a scenario. If you brush up against poison ivy you incur a very evident reaction. To remedy this we apply anti-itch cream or some other medical application. The problem with this approach is that we merely *alleviate* the **Effects** yet fail to *eliminate* the **Cause.** However, if we went into the yard and removed the plants this would directly attack the **Cause.** This cultivates a more enduring and sustainable change than the prior approach. A Revolutionary Mindset implies an intrinsic modification directed toward cause. Although, what begins as purely a revolution of the mind carries over into an evolution of lifestyle

This is part 2 of the Revolutionary mindset. (Here's where the brackets come in.) Revolutionary is a fascinating word in that it encompasses both words revolution and evolution. There is an interdependent mutuality between the mind and body. If we revolutionize our mind our body will evolve. As a firm believer in interpretation I am not going to try to force you upon a path you do not precisely fit. Instead I want you to pick your own path, where it leads is your choice. Choices are not always easy but take comfort in knowing they are yours and one of the few things we can still claim ownership of with absolute certainty. Remember, **your decisions are under your discretion.**

Lets start a Revolution, a Mindset Revolution! I like to think of this book as a study in the "science of <u>thought</u>." My request is simple, *change the way in which you think.* Remember though; **many simple things are not easy.**

By the end of this book you should be able to separate yourself from the masses because you patiently sat and contemplated life. I see so often people get caught in perpetual movement. Many of us live under the false pretenses that we must work harder to get ahead. My goal is not to prevent you from moving, but rather to ensure you are moving in the right direction. Revolt against the "norms," Evolve as a person and move in the direction you want to go!

Chapter 1:

Transformation Information

Before we may initiate our [r]evolutionary journey we must first develop a sense of understanding. After all **understanding is the beginning of resolution.** True, this book provides information, my aspiration however is that you extract much more. As mentioned in the *Preframing*, we need to properly prepare ourselves. Approached correctly this book could be transformative.

Lets briefly ponder information. According to *Websters* information is defined as: "knowledge that you get about something: facts or details about a subject." So information includes knowledge, and facts. However when thinking about knowledge and facts, we may ask "what constitutes knowledge?" or "what is considered fact?" The answer is largely subjective and not firmly grounded. Ask these questions to multiple people and receive various answers. This shows that delineating *information* as simply knowledge and facts is a loosely held definition.

Inspecting the two ideas in this chapter: Information and Transformation, one clear cut differentiation is this. Information is gathered within the brain, whereas transformation is an outward lifestyle change. Where information stays within the confines of our consciousness, transformation has an actionable affect on our lives. A [r]evolutionary mindset therefore involves much more than changing the way you think. It is a complete transformation from the inside out. Picture it this way:

Information = Manifestation/Transformation = Application

This means information always stays in our heads whereas transformation takes place on the outside.

Getting a grip on Information

As depicted earlier, information entailed knowledge and facts. I believe knowledge and facts are necessary components but do not represent the whole. Use this book as an example. It provides information. How? By the words within it, they deliver a message. Lets perform an even further autopsy. What are words? A collection of letters which we associate meaning. So what are letters? Letters are an accumulation of squiggles, which we bestow significance to. We use these squiggles to build words; words build sentences, sentences to paragraphs, to books, to the English language. Each of which provides information. Whether this information is interpreted the same is determined by the meaning we give to it. In that regard we may not all consider it to contain knowledge or facts. It does however contain an "order." All of information has order. The words on this page have an order of letters, the code on this computer, which I am typing, has an order of numbers, the clothes I am wearing have an order of thread fibers holding them together, etc. **All of life is order; much is imperfect order, but order nonetheless.** Look to nature for instance. Being out in nature is among my favorite activities. It is exquisitely soothing in an awe inspiring way. If we examine animals hunting, we don't view it as murder; we depict it as survival, the circle of life. Many times when I am out hiking I observe fallen trees or torn up plants, each of which are imperfect, yet still emulate perfection. The fallen trees add a serene realness to the environment, and will eventually become part of the land, as will the plants. This is the information of the world, the order. As humans we tend to have a ceaseless conviction to create order out of the chaos. We seek information and validate it in a quantifiable way. The same way we read this book based on pre-conceived notions of language, is the same manner in which we approach all of life.

Chapter 2:

The Hidden Super Power

At this point we have covered a few bases. First we emptied our mind, and then established purpose. Now lets talk strategy, HOW to approach this book. "How" (if you didn't notice by the capitalization) is the primary word we will focus on in this chapter. Before we hit "How" hard, it's imperative we understand something else first.

The Power of Questions

Questions are the roadmap to [R]evolutionizing our mindset. We must create the habit of asking ourselves more questions, questions, questions. Think of asking yourself questions as problem solving for your brain. After all, **thought is simply the process of asking and answering questions.** For each question asked, your brain immediately rummages for answers. Realize though we can ask both positive and negative questions. Some lift us up while others bring us down. "How can we begin to focus on the most beneficial questions?" Well! Lets use that question as an example. The good news is that by asking this we are already on the right track…. (Lets have some fun with words…) You may be asking "How are we on the right track?" How is How! Whaaaaaaaat???? Some of you are scratching your head; just hold your horses for a minute. Remember in the beginning of this chapter we talked strategy. We mentioned HOW we were going to implement our newfound mindset. The first way is by asking questions, more accurately, questions starting with "How." Begin to ask *yourself* more questions; asking *others* is great, although I believe true power lies in intrinsic uplifting questions. Think of a time when you did something difficult, maybe it was a physical activity like exercise or a difficult task. Perhaps it was an emotionally difficult decision such as quitting your job. I'm willing to bet you asked yourself a ton of questions. Lets use "quitting your job" as an example. You made the decision. Now the questions begin pouring in... "How should I approach this," "How can I find the best time," "How should I word it," "How much notice do I give?" This creates clarity and allows you to develop a clear-cut strategy. On the contrary many times our inner dialogue sounds more like this... "Is this really the right decision," "What will my co-workers think," "What will my friends think," "What if the conversation does not go well," "What if my boss does not like me anymore," "Will they recommend me for other jobs?" Notice the disempowerment of these questions, they will bury you in an emotional low and only ensure more difficulty in decision.

I have gathered much information on the amazing power of questions. Allow me to shed some light on this. Lets start with the granddaddy of all things personal development, Tony Robbins. He explains how our brains are servomechanisms, meaning they hunt down answers like a heat seeking missile. My goal is to show you how to move from asking yourself limiting question to empowering questions. Robbins has an answer for that too. His business is based on positive human change. One of his methods talks about focus, to quote him *"What we focus on we get more of."* Changing our quality of questions trickles down to what we are focusing on. Regarding the "quitting your job" scenario above we can choose to focus on the adversity of breaking up or the opportunity of starting fresh, each resulting in a different set of feelings or emotions. The amazing part is **all feelings are derivatives of our questions.**

Lets begin to ask our selves "QBQ's." *QBQ* is the title of a book I read, which stands for *"Question Behind the Question."* In this book, author John Miller writes about the questions we need to ask to avoid Victim mentalities, complaining, and procrastination. This fantastic quick read defines the QBQ as:

1. Questions that begin with "What" or "How" Not why, when, or who.

11

2. Contain an I, Not they, we, or you

3. Focus on action

Here is an example: "How am I going to approach my boss to announce my resignation?" Starts with how, contains an "I," and is indicative of action, this is a QBQ!

The criteria of Miller's book concentrates on building personal accountability. Asking QBQ'S energizes our thoughts and feelings. Our goal is to eliminate what John Miller calls IQ'S (Incorrect Questions) and replace them with self accountable QBQ'S.

If you are thinking, "How can I do that?" you are following along brilliantly. This is the last piece of the puzzle. Another read of mine was a more popular book entitled *Rich Dad Poor Dad.* Of the many profound ideas gathered from this book, among the most prominent had to be when author Robert Kiyosaki wrote about the paradigm shift from "I can't…" to "How can I…" For those unfamiliar, this book is classified as "financial literacy," however I like to think of it as financial psychology due to its relation to thinking. Throughout the text Robert talks about the discrepancies between average people and rich people. A typical thinking pattern for average people in a financial context is " I can't afford that" whereas rich people think "How can I afford that." This immensely simple yet insightful concept can create abundance in our lives if we choose to switch our thought process from "I can't" to "How can I."

The Mindset Disparity

Hopefully now you have attained a clearer understanding of the fundamentally vital importance of asking questions. Let us begin upon the path to creating measurable adjustments in our lives. One profound thought that has kept me going is this:

The only distinction between average people and millionaires is mindset, between average people and Olympians is mindset, average people and philanthropists is mindset. If you no longer wish to have an average mindset, cease to think averagely. Mindset is the singular disparity between our selves and our perception of success. Our mindsets consist of nothing more than a series of asked and answered questions. Ask yourself questions successful people are asking and you'll get answers successful people are getting.

Chapter 3:

Slaves of the System

These days everywhere we turn it seems we are part of a system. Systems surround us and are many times essential. However most of us unconsciously roam about these systems lacking purpose. This is what I am here to change. It's imperative that we develop a sense of self-awareness to avoid becoming slaves to the system. In a minute I am going to paint a picture of the typical, unconscious "wave-rider" if you will, but first lets cover some ground. We don't have to look far to see these systems: the religious systems, the political systems, governmental systems, school systems, family systems, work systems, it's as if everything we do essentially is a system. Hear me out; I'm not saying systems are wrong or that we shouldn't abide by them. What I am saying, on the contrary, is that we should devise a plan to conform to some but eradicate others. Currently it appears humans meander along without conscious realization. Allow me to paint a picture, imagine yourself in this situation: You have become deeply integrated into a system. Like a minion, you begin marching in a single file line modeling the crowd. The only sight you see is the back of a head. If the line turns right, you turn right, left, you turn left. You feel good about yourself because you are moving, **action is taking place, but you are not getting any *traction*.** There is no purpose driving your action, you are simply in a state of activity lacking a designated course. Were you to zoom out on this robotic society you would realize not only a free-will void, but also a circular march to nowhere. In a microcosm, it appears as if you are moving toward a destination when in reality you are simply *moving,* with no end in mind. In a futile attempt to "escape" your fate, you look down. With your chin slumped you notice your hands cuffed around your waist, with a chain proceeding down your leg to your ankles, which are also cuffed. This unfortunately is modern day reality for many. It's as if we are in self-inflicted proverbial debt due largely to a commitment of lifestyle. Typically the story continues with a long trudging of servitude for eternity. Locked in with no sense of recourse.

The Exception to the Rule

That being said I'd like to explore an alternative course of action. What if we were to conclude this story differently? Lets look at the exception to the rule. So there you are legs and arms bound following "Mr. Hamster Wheel" in front of you. You are sluggish and depressed, until one day you formulate a plan. This time you say to yourself "you know what, screw this, I'm out of here" and you hop out of line. Of course almost instantaneously, the "river rafters" in line begin shouting out to you such things as: "What are you doing, get back in line" "You can't do that, what're you crazy" "What is the matter with you, nobody leaves the line." At this point the temptations to hop back in and ride the river to infinite nowhere once again begin. You are now driven by a new purpose, you have a plan, and nothing can stop you. From your new position you obtain a unique perspective. **You've begun acting upon life instead of it acting upon you**. While walking around "exploring," you eventually stumble upon a waist high pole rooted in the ground. This is what you have been in search of. Jumping up as high as you can you throw your legs over top, landing in a seated position with one foot on each side of the pole. Cuffs are on one side, freedom on the other. You begin pulling with extraordinary might towards freedom, cuffs yanked taught around the pole until... SNAP!! The proverbial chain breaks. Immediately you rise to your unbound feet and without delay you begin running. Run run run run you become an unstoppable force with momentum and motivation. You are now moving, for once with purpose. After creating enough traction for yourself eventually your mission is accomplished. You create a key for your handcuffs. With your hands free you realize the power of the key. Now is the point in the journey where a choice must be made. You can do one of two things with the key. Maybe you choose to go around with it and unlock everybody's cuffs. This may

15

cause alleviation in the short term but in the long term it's likely they'll end where they started. Or you may teach those uninitiated to make a key of their own which more often than not leads to lasting change.

Obviously this story was a metaphor. It was my intent to make it so in order to allow individual interpretation. We as humans all possess an incredible power. This power has lain dormant for many years but is waiting patiently to be awakened from its slumber. The power to choose! Choice is what we have as human beings, it is our time to act upon the world, instead of having it act upon us. Get up go do it, don't find reasons, get results. **We can have reasons or results, but we can't have both.** Reasons are a manifestation of the brain, they are formed in the brain and stay there, results on the contrary are indicative of action. It is up to us to act, and to act for ourselves because there are not many things we have control over in this world, but we can control ourselves. This idea has been famously articulated in numerous ways; I like to sum it up in one sentence:

"We don't always have control over what happens to us, but we can always *decide* how we *choose* to respond to it."

Remember there are three different types of people in this analogy. The "Wave Riders" are those that go with the flow and are unconsciously in bondage/slavery to a system. The "One that got away" the person who makes a key but then keeps it for themselves and exploits others. Lastly the "Exception to the rule" who also makes a key but shares his knowledge and expertise with the world. Now its time to ask yourself, "Which one do I want to be?" So pick a system, it doesn't matter which but make it intentional purposeful and most importantly *your choice!*

Chapter 4:

Human Being Human

Everybody is born with specific genetics that make us human. Many times in modern culture we perceive individuality as a derivative singularly from genetics, this is a very limiting point of view. I believe humanity has had a proverbial veil pulled in front of their eyes. So we're clear, I do not have a degree in Genetics, Neuroscience, or Psychology but I have researched these topics. In my study of Genetics I came across a concept that brought clarity to my theory of human capabilities. The concept of inheritances, genetics teaches two types, biological and cultural. Biological inheritances describe the genetics presupposed within our DNA dictating eye color, hair texture, hair color, size of mouth, nose, ears, bone density, bone structure, height, weight, etc. Each of these distinctions are biological inheritances, our genetic make up. It seems many believe humanity is based solely on biological inheritances, however there is another equally if not more important piece to the puzzle. Cultural inheritances, these are inheritances based on, you guessed it, your culture. For instance the English language is a cultural inheritance, you and I know English because our culture demanded it. Other such capabilities like walking, whistling, snapping your fingers, or any such skill you have acquired are all cultural inheritances. This it seems is where most make incorrect assumptions.

Another of my studies, supporting the genetics conundrum, was in Neuroplasticity! SAY WHAT?! Neuroplasticity is simply the connections or links made inside of our bodies whenever we do something. This predicates from Neuro-Linguistic Programming, a method used in psychology in an attempt to "re-program" people. Success Coach Tony Robbins has done many studies in this field and has come up with his own method, which he calls "Neuro-Associative

Conditioning." FREEZE! Before your eyes roll into the back of your head let me help you grasp this. Breakdown!

Neuro= Brain, Associative= Links, Conditioning= over and over again.

So NAC is simply how our brain links what we do repeatedly. An extensive study of NAC is not needed for the sake of this read, however if you are interested in finding out more I recommend reading Tony Robbins' book *Awaken the Giant Within*.

Baring all this you may be asking yourself; "How can our brain make these links?" Congratulations you've asked the golden question! Our Brain makes these links based on what we already know. Think of these *"knowns"* as a support team. Each *known* or reference is a player on the team. It is each of these players that hold up and give validity to our beliefs. Imagine your brain as a giant excel spreadsheet. Each time we learn something it's placed on that spreadsheet. When we attempt to learn something new our brain fascinatingly finds a memory on that spreadsheet that is similar and links it to what we are trying to learn. **All of learning is simply linking the known with the unknown.**

We will return to Genetics and neuroplasticity briefly. I wanted to give you an initial "crash-course" so we can be on the same frequency so to speak. When approaching these topics for study I frequently asked the loaded question; "Where do these *"knowns"* come from and can they be changed?" My answer is not Earth Shattering, although it did deliver much clarity and a better understanding of people. Remember: **understanding is the beginning of resolution**. If you find yourself in an un-resolved situation the first step is always to *understand* what went wrong. For instance: If you're sailing a ship and spring a leak you wouldn't just start filling in cracks blindly, you must first find the hole, and *understand* where to fill in. The same holds true for intrinsic "leaks." Now back to my question: "Where do these *"knowns"* come from and can they be changed?" my answer: **The 3"E's"** They are:

Environment
Experience
Education

These are the 3 things that shape our lives after biology is thrown into place. They make up the majority of our cultural inheritances. Most amazing is the fact that these three factors are largely under our *own* control.

Lets break them down:

Environment:
Environment is always listed first because the other two "E's" are built off of this one. Our environment is all around us and includes much more than just our visual observations. Environment could be defined as space and all within it. Remember we have 5 senses, many times people associate environment as visual observation. In reality our environment is anything we interact with through one or more of our 5 senses. *Websters* defines environment as: Surroundings, all the conditions etc. surrounding and affecting the development of an organism. For me the phrase "organism development" stood out. As I pondered I came to realize this definition is applicable to pretty much every life scenario. We are all "organisms," living things.

Environment plays a large role in our personal development, it's anything we can see, smell, hear, taste, or touch. Each of these interactions assists in our development as people. Environment is always an outward look. Typically all outward life is our environment.

When we focus on the outward we see the environment, however when we focus on the inward we get....

Experience:

This is a fun one. Immediately you may find your mind tracking down words related to experience. Words like: event, situation, circumstance, scenario, etc. Each provides an accurate description. Stated differently an experience is anything we live through. Our experiences are much more direct and personal than our environment. In contrast to environment, experience involves emotion. Experience described in a single word could be: Feeling. Among our life experiences each derive a feeling, some good some bad, regardless emotion is typically present. Our environments formulate our experiences and our experiences formulate us. Environment as previously asserted refers to our outward world, experiences manifest inwardly, involving a present emotional state. The final area from which individuality is spawned arises within the brain...

Education:

The third and final E represents Education. As stated education originates in the brain, although does not remain permanently affixed. Lets observe the process of education from a physiological level. Much of the information displayed in this chapter I received from the book *Emotional Intelligence* by Daniel Goleman. Goleman describes neurologically how our brain works in response to outward stimuli. Two key terms we need to understand are: neocortex & amygdala. These are both anatomical parts of the brain with distinctly specific functions. Amygdala controls emotions and neocortex controls thought. For our sake the amygdala is used in Experiences whereas the neocortex is used in Education. Education particularly focuses on thought where experiences rely on emotion. This simple notion creates a vast depth of clarity between each of these two E's.

To recap, individuality is largely created due to our 3E's. Our environment consists of the outside world, space and everything within it. Experiences manifest inwardly and are derived from our emotions. Education is based primarily on our thoughts, they allow us to grow and evolve as humans.

Chapter 4.1: Knowns and Unknowns

Lets look back at education, when you heard this I would venture to guess one word came to mind, Knowledge. This is an awesome word! Have you ever thought about what "knowledge" really means? Lets see if we can find its meaning. I need you to help me with this, are you ready?

Knowledge

Lets work together to crack the knowledge code. Here is what I need you to do, examine this word closely, look at it very precisely, visualize it in your head and break it down letter by letter. See anything?

Let me tell you what I found. But be warned this finding is so groundbreaking you may possibly hear my mind blowing. When initially examining the word *knowledge* I actually found <u>TWO</u> words, BOOM! Bet you didn't see that coming. All right I admit, not that mind blowing, but I'm sure the suspense was killing you. This is my find:

Know Ledge

Isn't it amazing what a millimeter of space can do?
Now we have some working capital, lets keep going!

KNOW   **LEDGE**

I took this finding one step further. Maybe I cheated a little but I like to think of it as improvising, I added the letter "N"

KNOW   **N**   **LEDGE**

So together it looks like this:

Known-Ledge

BOOOOO YA!

Knowledge is nothing more than our known-ledge. To make sense of my rambling, picture this in your head: "You are standing atop an enormous cliff. Glancing over the ledge, the cliffs expanse remains "UNKNOWN" to you. However, your feet remain firmly grounded, this you "KNOW." For countless miles behind you lies solid ground." In this analogy the ground represents the *known* and the cliff the *unknown*. We, metaphorically, are standing on the ledge of what we know and don't know. As we acquire more knowledge the base of the cliff ascends like an elevator. This creates more solid ground (knowns), which allow us to reach a new ledge. This cycle perpetually repeats upon itself without cease.

Hopefully this description helped clarify the knowledge dilemma. We only know so much, we have limited solid ground to stand on, after that we are either plummeting to an unknown location or working to acquire more knowledge/cultivate more ground.

Chapter 4.2: Brick by Brick

Knowledge is essential in the education puzzle. That being said, education entails much more than just knowledge, it is what makes us who we are. Education is built from the other two "E's" and we as people encompass all three E's in specifically distinctive ways. Lets look at these distinctions:

Imagine each E as a brick, now bricks can have multiple meanings. You can throw it through a window, or use it to build a hospital. Either way is your choice.

Everyone is designed from the same mortar and bricks (the 3E's), although assembly varies immensely. Individuals have many differences, for instance, you may like chocolate, I like vanilla, I am left-handed; pretty much everyone else is right handed (Lefties unite!!) You get the point. Despite our differences much of our structure is the same; for the most part we are all flesh, bones, blood, and water. There are points in life that congregate us, and points that separate us; most notably of these are three scenarios (lucky number 3 I guess) they are:

1. Order
2. Repetition
3. Intensity

Order:

Lets look at order. The order in which information is acquired fluctuates from individual to individual. For instance, have you ever known that person who just seemed to pick up skills quickly and accurately with pretty much any endeavor? What would you most likely say about them? "They're lucky," "That's just how they're "WIRED"... More importantly what would you say about yourself? "I can't do that," "Why can't I be as lucky as them," "If only I could do what they do, then I would be happy." At this precise moment you have instantly relinquished control and made yourself inferior. This is not a revolutionary mindset; it's a limiting mindset. You may be thinking these

24

circumstances are based on biological inheritances you would be partially correct. Yes there are people with unique dispositions that acquire skills more quickly, however this is a microscopic piece of a gargantuan puzzle. It is my belief there is no such thing as luck, your choices determine your lifestyle. Also I do not believe people are "wired" or "programmed." By simply changing our 3E's we begin to forge a life of our choice.

We all learn at different paces, not to say one order is right or wrong, but it's important to understand. Think of Children: some babies learn to walk sooner than others, as they grow reading and writing develops at different intervals, etc. Do note I am not saying humans are 100% a result of the 3E's, however they play a large role.

Repetitions:

In the beginning of this chapter I mentioned "Neuro associative conditioning." The vital element to "NAC" is "conditioning." For instance: I have begun learning to play guitar. As you play the strings wear out and need to be replaced. When putting new strings on they are so loose you end up having to tune the guitar multiple times until the strings become *conditioned* to stay in tune for longer periods of time. The same is true with our lives; to stay "in tune" we need to condition ourselves. The easiest way to condition your life on your terms is to change your 3E's to mirror your desires.

Conditioning is important, but retention is key. Think about learning a subject or hobby. The more you practice (repeat) the better you become. Increased repetitions lead to more accessible retention. Along with order, repetitions are fundamental in human assembly. The order in which you receive information and how often that information is repeated determines much of your life. We have covered order and repetition, however one more factor remains...

Intensity:

Have you ever had a tragic moment in your life?
Now how do you feel?

I'll bet when you recalled this moment two things happened.
1. Your mood INSTANTLY changed, and you began to feel the way you felt when this tragic moment occurred.
2. You remembered the moment vividly and intently.
    Allow me to ask another question:

Have you ever had a moment in your life of sheer beauty, a moment with such immense passion and commitment that you wanted to stay there forever?
How do you feel now?

Once again I'll bet the same two responses occurred. These questions describe moments of emotional intensity. We all have these moments; they can be big like the above scenarios, or something small yet holding intrinsic significance. Either way we're bound to respond similarly to the two ways discussed above. Do note, these moments don't have to be catastrophic or groundbreaking they can be something as simple as laughter. Laughter is one of the highest-level emotions we are given. Have you ever had a good friend of yours tell a hilarious joke that made you feel like you were going to laugh for days? Think about it, I'm sure you can remember a time distinctly. How many of you took that joke and started telling it to your friends? Ever wondered why you remembered it? Laughter! Laughter is an amazing emotion.
    The point of this section and these questions is to help you understand emotional intensity. Any time we are subjected to a situation of high emotional intensity whether it's a wedding, funeral, car accident, or haunted house, our brains become immediately imprinted with this series of events. The key to emotional intensity is that we remember these events. These events of high emotional intensity aid human development. How many stories have you heard about someone who

26

lived through a catastrophic event and then developed conditions from it? Post Traumatic Stress Disorder (PTSD) is the perfect example. Typically found in military veterans, PTSD is a condition associated with previous situations of high emotional stress that can be recalled and recreated almost congruently.

Anytime we recall these feelings we are using that moment to shape our present and future beliefs. The three main factors, which most prominently shape our 3E construction, are order, repetition, and emotional intensity. Our life is simply our rendition of these inheritances.

Chapter 4.3: Fish, Geese, Lions, Monkeys, and You!

This chapter is the core of this book. If I leave you with nothing else, go with this. The 3E framework is a collection of knowledge I uncovered from reading other books like: *Awaken the Giant Within: Tony Robbins, The Power of full Engagement: Jim Loehr and Tony Schwartz, and Emotional Intelligence: Daniel Goleman.* In particular these 3 books, as well as many others, helped to shape the entire framework of this book, mainly this chapter. I claim none of this knowledge as my own, but merely my adaptation of the greats which live before me. As Isaac Newton said:

"If I have seen further than others, it is by standing upon the shoulders of giants."

My message to you is simple. **Do not ask whether something is right or wrong; ask whether your actions are getting you closer or further away from your plan.** Right or wrong is a totally subjective way of thinking. Answers differ based on multiple factors. Think of hunting, is hunting right or wrong? Ask hunters and you'll get one answer, ask non-hunters and you'll get another. What about eating meat; is that right or wrong? Or keeping a gun in the house, from a moral or ethical standpoint are these questions right or wrong? You'll receive various answers depending upon whom you ask. In that respect I will not recommend one correct path to follow with all kinds of rules and regulations. What I will do however is teach you to fish. I hope to provide you with much more than just a golden egg of information. My intent is to show you where to find the geese that lay golden eggs.

Your 3E's are yours and you are amazing in so many ways. The beauty of the 3E's is we can change and manipulate them freely. Yes the past is in the past and to quote one of my favorite Disney characters of all time:

"The past can hurt, but we can either run from or learn from it, now what are you going to do?" –Rafiki, The Lion King.

In this life there is no succeeding or failing there is only succeeding or learning. Learn from your past and move onward unto victory because although we don't always have control over what happens to us we can always control how we choose to respond to it. So chisel your life into whatever you want it to be. If you're upset with something change your E's. Turn your life into one of empowerment because you are strong and most importantly capable. Nobody on the face of this planet is responsible for your happiness except yourself. So be happy, be alive, be the person who you want to be. Live life to the fullest, for this is the true essence of human being human.

To victory my friends!

Chapter 5:

The Value of Life

All values are intrinsic qualities that aid in the fabrication of humans. They are constructed based on our 3E's. Last chapter I briefly alluded to our brains being like spreadsheets lets elaborate on this. In our minds we continuously file our beliefs within a proverbial spreadsheet. Beliefs are nothing more than a feeling of assurance. Take our beliefs a step further and we have values. Our values are strong, rigid, and ironclad, they determine what we believe in. In regards to the spreadsheet analogy values would be listed at the top with corresponding beliefs beneath them. Picture it this way: across the top row of your spreadsheet are your values (V's) listed side by side. Beneath these are sets of similar beliefs (B's) here is an example:

The V/B Spreadsheet

V	V	V	V	V	V
B B	BB BB	BB B B	B B B B	BB BB	B B

In any given situation our V's and B's are either aligned or misaligned. We have subconscious rules governing our V's and B's. These determine our responses which affect our entire decision making process. Typically when our V's and B's are misaligned we become indecisive, whereas when they are aligned decision comes easily. When we are more aware of our V's and B's better decisions can be made. Now days in my opinion many value the wrong things, lets look at an example.

I am going to speak for all the guys out there (This still applies to you ladies so listen up.) It's Saturday morning; you're off from work. You wake up, get dressed, come downstairs and adjourn to the living room. As you sit down in "Your" chair, and turn on the television you notice your spouse is gone. You have the house to yourself, YES! However something is inevitably wrong... while watching TV you notice you're looking into the same tube television "Fat screen" you've watched for years. You *need* a new TV. In your head the justification battle begins and you begin to rationalize. You have been researching for months waiting for this fateful moment. Like a tiger stalking its prey you pounce... hop in the car and B-Line to the electronic store. You pull in, enter the store, grab a sales associate by his lapels, drag him to the TV you want, point and say THIS ONE! When your significant other returns... I'll let you decide the outcome. The point is as humans we can justify purchasing liabilities and take the time and trouble to inform ourselves on frivolous matters. Yet we can't seem to place as much time and energy into our future. Our physical, mental, financial, and spiritual futures never seem to have plan, they kind of just happen. Planning for our future requires a similar approach to the example above. (Ladies this goes for your purchases of shiny things as well.) In order to produce the results we want later we need to be purposeful with what we are doing now. What we do now is a reflection of what we will get in the future. **Later is created today.**

In modern day this type of justification is seen so fervently. People are provoked by *feeeeeeeeeeeelings* so much that emotions often cloud our purchasing judgment. Due to the incessant influx of media we are in a constant search of truly important values. Regardless, we rationalize our *need* for "things." To keep the theme of this book I will

31

not recommend one specific set of values that every person should believe in. Humans are too complex for a singular set of rules. The underlying key to this chapter is to think for your self. One of the most basic yet profoundly powerful pieces of advice I can give you is to **think ahead**. So many times people get caught in the moment. In *Chapter 3: Slaves of the System,* we talked about being stuck in a single file line only able to see 3 inches ahead. These chains need to be broken if we wish to see a [R]evolutionary change in our lives. If we establish the habit of thinking ahead we yield dominion over the shortsighted.

Thinking to the future is important but considering we live in the present we must also think "here and now." Note, this does not mean, "go with the flow," but rather a realization and acceptance of our current position. I have found that many times removal from a situation allows for clearer understanding. There is typically a better view from the outside in. By simply slowing down we have the opportunity to choose the best response. Notice I said respond, not react. A response involves thought and training whereas a reaction is instinctual and instantaneous. Lets develop a sense of responding as apposed to reacting.

As you begin to listen proactively, people's thoughts and intentions will appear more evident. You'll begin to see typical thinking patterns and discern peoples true values and beliefs. Which will help you perceive the modern myths of the world, lets explore a few!

Chapter 5.1 Modern Mythology

I personally am a big fan of Greek Mythology and know many of the characters and stories. Although much of mythology is obviously fantasy I do believe many stories serve as a great metaphor for life. If we examine the Greeks in particular and their take on mythology one thing they did very well with each of their stories was answer questions. "Why is it raining?" for example, Greek Mythologies answer: "The mighty god of the sky Zeus has cursed the sky with thunderbolts," "Why did that man die?" "Lord Hades claimed him for the underworld etc. This holds true throughout Greek Mythology. This gave the Greeks clarity and something to point to even if it was utterly ridiculous. From a modern perspective these ancient beliefs seem outrageously insane. Remember though only a short while ago everybody KNEW the earth was flat, before that everybody KNEW the earth was the center of the universe. The point I stress is that as a species we are insatiably compelled to find an answer at any length. In *Chapter 2: The Hidden Super Power* we spoke about how our brain will hunt down answers for whatever we ask of it. Typically it will give us the answers we have heard before. In the case of Greek Mythology, people believed in the God's because it was so widely spread and talked about across the land that everybody, unconsciously sometimes, adopted this thinking pattern. We act very much the same today in our unquenchable search for clarity. Everybody on this planet needs to be led. We all need something to follow. Every single solitary living breathing human organism is in search of one thing... A feeling. **We are, at our most basic level nothing more than the way we feel.** Physiologically as humans we change constantly and consistently, the dead skins cells on the outer layer of our bodies are continuously being replaced as well as many internal functions. My goal is to help you to change psychologically as well. Lets take a look at some of the modern myths being thrown around:

> ➤ Reading books makes you smarter: Although this may seem contradictory (considering you're reading it in a

book) lets explore further! I have heard my whole life "You need to read books if you want to be smarter." I believe this statement to be partially true, although a key aspect is missing. Most view reading books in a black and white manner, reading is good, not reading is bad. I believe this view is limiting and there are many *Shades of Grey* involved with reading. Reading in fact for much of my life has been a *Chamber of Secrets,* which I only recently explored. I do agree much can be learned when we read, however this statement presents the false notion that if we read our IQ will instantly increase. I believe **reading the right books** will make you smarter. Books that focus on an area of growth, books that were written for learning. However reading for entertainment is still a viable option though doesn't present the same benefits of reading something of substance. Lets keep going!

➤ Knowledge is power: No Way Jose! Knowledge is not power, knowledge is knowledge, and how many of you know somebody that is knowledgeable yet still powerless? Raise your hand. Think of knowledge as a bullet, by itself it's useless; it needs a gun to create power. That "gun" is application.

"Knowing is not enough, we must apply." – Bruce Lee

Application is perhaps the most crucial element to creating power. After all **knowledge without application is as useless as no knowledge at all.** It's easy to know what is considered right and wrong. Applying this to everyday life, however, is the challenging part. Although sometimes "in order to achieve success we must sacrifice." Cease to think knowledge is power, but rather understand **applied knowledge is power**. Just remember that application is only sufficient if we apply ourselves in the right direction. Which brings us our next myth.

➢ Right or Wrong: This was mentioned briefly in *Ch. 4.3 Fish, Geese, Lions, Monkeys, and You!* Lets expand upon it now. How many times in life have you heard; "do this because it's right," or "don't do this because it's wrong?" Countless I am sure. As noted in Ch. 4.3 the problem lies in the fact that right and wrong are subjective ideas with varying perceptions. My suggestion was to not ask yourself whether something is right or wrong, but rather ask: **"Is this bringing me closer or further away from my plan?"** The prerequisite to this new pattern of thinking being do I have a plan? Give yourself a direction and purpose, something to aim for. Create congruency in your life by making everything you do in accordance with your plan. Before we conclude this topic though there is one caveat I must leave you with. Understand the number one, most quintessential rule to having a plan... things **WILL NOT** go according to plan. Having a plan also means learning to become adaptable and malleable. This way when things begin to chart off course (and they *will* chart off course) you will be able to move yourself back to the fast track. Lets look at the next myth that needs debunking...

➢ Time Management = Success: It's heard all the time, "If you want to be successful learn how to manage your time." This "buzz phrase" has become so immersed in society that people blindly follow it with minimal understanding. Let's look further. Claiming to be too busy during a day is never a statement dictating a lack of time but rather a lack of purpose. As we know a day has 24 hours. Yet, armed with this knowledge many still wind up in a crazed whirlwind of angst. When confronted with a challenge "the blame game" inevitably begins "I don't have enough time" "I am too busy" " I can't do that now!" Instantaneously time is seen as the culprit and we enter into a delusional state thinking we can correct something uncorrectable. Instead shift your paradigm and view purpose as the culprit, not time. Your days should be purposeful. The great news about days is they hold few surprises. Barring cataclysmic events we know they're 24 hours. We know days entail eating, sleeping, and using the restroom. Purpose as stated earlier is the missing link. As apposed to <u>wasting</u> time figuring out how you ran out of time, why not <u>invest</u> time purposefully planning your day. **Do not waste; invest!** By intentionally writing out your days you can create more efficiency in your life. **Intention is nothing more than purposeful energy exertion.** Make the change to give your day purpose and watch as this carries over into weeks, months, years, and ultimately destiny!

Time is an uncontrollable, but what is controllable is energy. We can always control the energy we choose to put forth at any given time. Lets shift our focus from time management to energy management. Energy management, in my opinion, should become the modern buzz phrase of society. The saying should go: **"If you want to be successful learn how to manage your energy."** This more accurately describes what is being managed. Sit down and make your day intentional, let me know how much time you can find?

➤ Honesty is the best policy: When we hear this phrase what is typically the case? Somebody makes an honest statement and then throws this phrase out attempting to sound clever. At this point both people may chuckle a little and then walk away. The issue herein lies that neither person stops and thinks about what was said. They take it as truth and move on. Conversely many times honesty is not the best policy. Look at our culture; often we neglect to tell the truth because we want no hard feelings. We seek a constant societal equanimity; therefore cease to always be honest. So we proceed by stretching, twisting, or avoiding the truth to abstain from hurting other's feelings. Yet these same people twisting the truth are saying honesty is the best policy? The truth is most people are only honest when it's convenient for them. Lets look at two quick examples. This first example is for men. You come home from work or school and your mother or wife is waiting for you at the front door with a new hairstyle. They ask your opinion and (In unison now men) "It looks lovely" On the outside we attempt to awkwardly express appreciation, on the inside however.... IS YOUR HAIRDRESSER BLIND!! Ladies here is a similar analogy (and by the way your hair looks beautiful.) Your dad or husband decided to shop alone today and bought a shirt that he believed took his "cool status" from Ehhhhh to EXCELLENT! As fate would have it you pull up the driveway and there he is with his new purchase slung around his torso. You exit the car and he approaches with the dumbfounded gestures and question "Guess what I did today??" You play along asking "What?" "I GOT A NEW SHIRT!!" he says. Your response (in unison now ladies) "It looks lovely." I digress. Hopefully these analogies helped to give you a sense of realism when it comes to our habits of honesty. It can be more rightfully said that: **Honesty is the best policy, until somebody is honest about you.** Did you ever notice that when we're truly honest about someone they often assume a defensive posture? They attempt to alleviate the blame from themselves and place it elsewhere. All this to say lets truly assess a situation before we start throwing around phrases we don't totally understand. Lets examine two more quick myths!

➤ Split your focus: It's heard frequently that splitting our focus helps to increase productivity. I beg to differ. This phrasing in my opinion is many times misleading. A more appropriate phrase would be to **divide your focus.** Think of it this way, splitting your focus would be like trying to read the left page of this book with your left eye while simultaneously reading the right page with your right eye. Think of having a rope with split ends forming a Y shape. Your focus is split in two apposing directions, neither receiving as much focus as the initial "rope." Instead of splitting your focus divide it and focus on one thing at one time to ensure maximum efficiency!

➤ It is what it is: By now you should be capable of seeing the holes in this logic yourself. As per the tune of this entire book the fundamental basis is that WE are in control. Each of us has the power to control ourselves physically, mentally, emotionally, and spiritually with enough understanding and desire. "It is what it is" is not what it is; **It is what you make it.** So whatever you do, make it a good one!

This was merely a sampling of a few modern myths out there. The underlying point being when we step back and take time to truly think the solution often presents itself. Look around and see what other modern myths you can find! Take an approach of knowledge and where-with-all so that you may truly begin to [R]evolutionize your thoughts, actions, and most importantly... lives!

Chapter: 6

Funneled down to Goals

It has become fact that no self-help book would be complete without a chapter on goal setting. With this I would like to provide my rendition and present new insights regarding goals. First lets define a goal. Here I am not going to use *Webster's,* I believe a goal is too personal for a definition confined within a dictionary. Goals are anything you aspire to achieve. Those who have pursued anything worthwhile will understand the path to accomplishment is painted with treacherous obstacles. Without proper ammunition, these challenges appear as insurmountable undertakings. Fret no more I am here to set you straight.

Traversing Mount Achievement

You may have heard the S.M.A.R.T. goal setting principle or the BE-DO-HAVE principle and perhaps others. Regardless your pain-staking climb up Mount Achievement is met with ineptitude each time. I believe this to be for a multitude of reasons. Largely in part due to the fact that many people have misconceptions about what a goal actually is. From my collection of research on multiple goal setting principles I have devised a solution that will [R]evolutionize the way we view our entire universe! Okay not really but it will give goal setting much more clarity.

Lets break goals down. When you first spawn an idea you generate an image in your head, which evokes a feeling. This is a dream; you have a dream of traversing Mount Achievement. But dreams alone will not bring you to the apex. Upon your first scaling attempt you will likely take a spill and come crashing down with exceptional force. Should you choose to rise up after this head over heels mishap, you may decide to delve further into your dream. You will begin to put boundaries around it and start to more clearly define exactly what you want. Here our dream turns into a vision. A second time we put on the

40

harness, strap on the gear, grasp the rope and begin our ascent. With relentless perseverance we climb, higher than before, only to realize our obstacle is much bigger than we initially thought. This is the usual tipping point where we enter a state of paralysis. We do nothing and are encountered with an overwhelming feeling of anxiousness. Some remain paralyzed forever staring blankly at this "out of bounds" vision never to rise up. Others begin their descent back down to earth with the false notion that all hope is lost. The few visionaries that remain harnessed and prepared devise a plan. They view their dream with great clarity. Making, as precisely as they can, this manifestation into a personified reality. They establish a goal by taking this vision and adding more specificity and clarity to it. By doing this they have reached the adolescence of goal setting. Empowering questions begin to flood their mind, such as: What Do I really want? Why do I Want it? How can I get it? What is my best course of action? This continues until they have a rigidly defined plan of attack. Our final step is to take this goal from manifestation to externalization. Manifestation to externalization is simply a seventeen dollar way of saying write it down. There is a particular relief that comes from writing goals down. Now back to our climb. A conviction of power forms from within which carries us to the pinnacle of Mount Achievement.

The Goal Funnel

Lets put this eloquent analogy into more digestible terms. Here is a common example. Currently I perceive the world as being in a "boom" state, not a baby boom, but rather a fitness boom. It is evident that health and fitness have taken the world by storm with gyms, community centers, fitness facilities, and the like popping up on nearly every corner. With this notion in mind I think it's fair to say that for many, physical fitness or even vitality are among our top priorities. However that being said why do so many still remain overweight and out of shape? A majority of reasons come into play. One pressing matter is due largely to the fact that many people are dreamers, not goal setters. Some of you may be thinking, " What are you talking about, I want to get in shape, that's my goal!" Sorry to burst your bubble but that's not a goal, its a dream. Lets pretend for the sake of this drill this is what you want.

"I want to get in shape"

You are telling yourself this and believe it to be a goal, yet you consistently fall short. Perhaps you believe this is because you don't have the time to work out, or the money, or the confidence, etc. We are missing some key components. Let me ask you some questions, what is your definition of "in shape?" Do you know exactly what results you want and how to get them? These questions are meant to encourage you to place specificity on your goal. Does "in shape" mean lose weight, gain muscle, increase flexibility, etc.? For the sake of this example let's say it means lose weight, now lets specify that, how much weight; 5, 10,15, 20 pounds? You have to decide but once again to follow this example we'll say 15 pounds. Now we are beginning to pour some concrete. Lets re-assess your dream now and see the progress. We went from "I want to get in shape" to " I want to lose 15 pounds." Now we poured the cement, lets smooth it out. We discovered the *what*, now lets uncover *how* you are going to lose 15 pounds? You could join a gym, go to a fitness club, or take martial arts or yoga classes. Regardless we need to pick one for our example or I will never be able to finish this book. Lets say you want to join your local gym to lose 15 pounds. Not bad, but we still have a few loose ends. When? We need to establish a time line for our goal or else it will go on forever. Whatever time frame you pick my recommendation is to make it realistic yet challenging. Lets say 3 times a week for 6 months. Lastly we need to be aware of the language we use. By simply changing one word enormous difference will be made. Change the word "want." I want to achieve this vs. I am going to achieve this, which one sounds more likely to happen? Now we have created a solid piece of concrete that can easily be walked on without caving in. Examine your progression, we started with a dream: *"I want to get in shape"* then we chiseled away to a vision: *"I want to lose 15 pounds"* and finally forged a goal: *" I am going to the gym 3x a week to lose 15lbs in 6 months."* I have created an info-graphic to give an easy reference of what was explained.

The Goal Funnel:

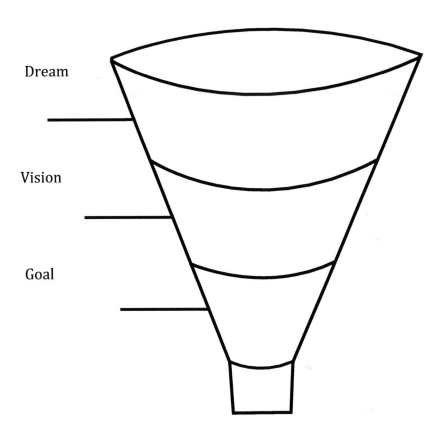

Dream

Vision

Goal

Notice at the top, the most broad section, we have dreams. As it begins to taper inward we move to a vision and finally the small end is the goal itself.

Now lets plug in our goal:

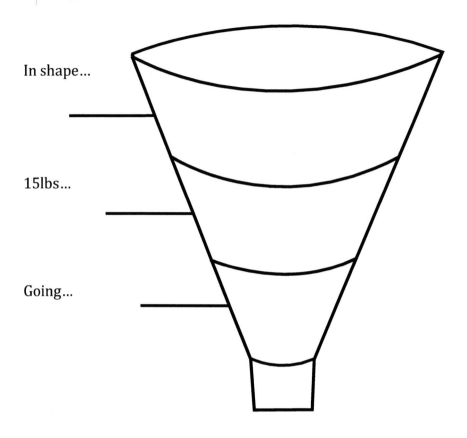

In shape...

15lbs...

Going...

At the top would go "I want to get in shape" your dream. As we taper inward it turns into "I want to lose 15 pounds." Finally it gets funneled down to the goal: "I am going to the gym 3 days a week so I can lose 15 pounds in 6 months."Armed with this knowledge we now have the capability to traverse Mount Achievement.

* Do not forget though after all this to write your goal down, without this step it's almost inevitable you'll come tumbling down the mountain again. To help you out I provided a blank goal funnel at the end of this book that you can fill in for yourself *

Next time you tell yourself you want to do something funnel it down to a goal and when you reach the pinnacle don't forget to place a copy of this book at the top!

Chapter 7:

Join the Revolution!

What a rollercoaster ride this has been! Congratulations, we are officially approaching the climax of this book, there are only a few stones left unturned. So far we have covered much ground, we emptied our mind, revolted into an evolved lifestyle, transformed our lives, discovered our hidden super power, freed ourselves from the slavery imposed by life systems, came to a realization of the 3E's, debunked modern mythology, and finally funneled down our goals. Let's speak of another life defying truth that will shape and empower our future. Freedom!

The word freedom always seems to be thrown around in a "lacking" sense, as if it's something missing from our lives. I believe, similar to *Ch.2 The Hidden Super Power,* how we had a super power within us all along, the same holds true with freedom. In truth, *nobody* wants "freedom" they want **everlasting freedom,** freedom on their timeframe. Think about it in terms of this book, did you have the freedom to purchase it yes or no? Did you have the freedom to read it (even though I persuaded you to keep going throughout) yes or no? Did you have the freedom to decide not to do either of these things yes or no? When you look deeper you will discover freedom has been there all along, just for many it has not lived up to your expectations. The greatest triumph in this is that we all have the freedom to change our expectations. Do not go through life expecting freedom to show up one day. Use the freedom you have to live the life you want!

The Millimeter Milestone

Remember the metaphor of the journey we spoke of. Designate yourself a finish line but take joy in the process of commuting. If you need to make a change to your life plan I have fantastic news. However far away you think your dream life truly is, if you look closely you may notice you are only a millimeter away. Sometimes a minor adjustment can make a world of difference. Take this book for example. If I handed you a gun and asked you to shoot a hole in this book directly down the center, it would be very easy. * Please make sure the gun is aiming away from you * Even if you didn't take time to do calculations to make your shot precise the center could still be hit. Now place this book 100 yards away. If the barrel of the gun is off by even one millimeter, by the time the bullet reaches 100 yards it will have missed the book completely. So sometimes in life in order to achieve desired results all it takes is one millimeter of change to create miles of difference. This, my friends is the Millimeter Milestone.

For you and me both this has been quite the undertaking. As a first time writer I never thought I would make it this far. Upon seeing this book come to fruition I can say with absolute certainty this was one of the most challenging yet rewarding experiences of my life to date. That being said this is certainly not the last time we will be meeting. As the reader I am sure you were uncertain what was in store, but I am glad you took this wild ride with me and I hope you continue on your journey toward a [R]evolutionary Mindset!

Chapter 8

The Road to Find Out...

(One final note)

One of my favorite songs is a Cat Stevens tune called *"The Road to Find Out."* This makes an appropriate title, because it's a great song, but also because it accurately describes where you are right now. Approaching the climax of this [R]evolution means you are stepping on the road to find out. Metaphorically you are on a road, you don't know where it will take you, but you feel encouraged to traverse onward. With this strange barren place lying before you I leave you with a few pieces of advice to make your travels easier. Remember to always think long term while on the road. Short sightedness will leave you just that, short. Be resourceful and take opinions from many on the path, but remember the final choice is always your own.

May your journey begin! You are now fully prepared to [R]evolutionize your life. March upon your path toward a re-invigorated future, and achieve victory my friends for the reward will always be well worth the journey!

- Fred Posimo

My top 10 Book Recommendations

As some of you know I recently developed an affinity towards reading. I mainly read self-help, personal development, and financial literacy. Most of this writing comes from other books I have read. Here is my list of the top 10 books I highly recommend to each of you with a short description of each.

1. *"Rhinoceros Success"* – Scott Alexander:
(Self/help, personal growth, success.) A short, super easy read, quirky, fun, creative with a fantastic message. With less than 100 pages this book is applicable to all ages, kids, teens, adults. It's about making life a success.

2. *"The Question behind the Question"*(QBQ) - John G. Miller:
(Personal Accountability) Another short, easy read, simple, clear, concise, well written and fun to travel through. It talks about the power of questions.

3. *"The Power of Full Engagement"* – Tony Schwartz & Jim Loehr:
(Business/ Self Help) Great read, brings much clarity to the discussion of energy expenditure and renewal. Easy read, a bit longer than the first two books, but worth the time.

4. *"The Total Money Makeover"* – Dave Ramsey:
(Personal Finance/ Self-Help) This was the first book I ever read and the catalyst for my reading expedition. It's a fantastically simple and easy to understand book on money, not sophisticated or complex, just concise and poignant.

5. *"Rich Dad Poor Dad"* – Robert Kiyosaki:
Sticking with financial literacy. (Read this after the Total money makeover, it will make more sense.) It presents a great paradigm shift on modern money perceptions.

6. *"The Cashflow Quadrant"* –Robert Kiyosaki:
(Part 2 of *"Rich Dad Poor Dad."*) Brings immense clarity to the working world, with an emphasis on income generators and an easy to understand guide on the pros and cons of each.

7. *" The E-Myth"* – Michael Gerber:
(Business) This is the quintessential business book for any current or aspiring entrepreneur. If you own or plan on owning a business and have not read this book you are missing out! Makes business practices simple and emphasizes the importance of systemization.

8. *"Awaken the Giant Within"* – Tony Robbins:
(Psychology) I am a raving fan of Tony's, his teachings are unparalleled and his passion is second to none. If you have not read his books or listened to his teachings check him out.

9. *"#Human"* – Chris Matakas:
(Philosophy, self-awareness, & self-actualization) It has presented a paradigm shift in my life I never knew existed before. I happen to know the author. Professor Chris Matakas is one of the best Jiu-Jitsu instructors I have had the privilege of working with as well as an accomplished author. Thank you Professor, you are one of my inspirations for writing.

10. *"The 7 Habits of Highly Effective People"* -Steven Covey:
Considered one of the best self-help books of all time I had to include it in my top ten. A little longer read than most but shares valuable insights into making the most of what we have and developing habits that will empower and rejuvenate your life.

I would love to keep this list going on forever but within the confines of these pages it is simply not feasible. Fortunately technology has afforded us the opportunity to continue this list. I gave you my ten I want to know yours.

If you have an **Instagram** account take pictures of the books which have most impacted you and post them with the **#revobooks.** Together lets start a community of great books for everybody to read.

About the Author

Fred Posimo is a 21-year-old martial arts instructor at Extreme Karate and Fitness. He has developed a passion for learning and self-improvement. Fred chose self-education over a college degree; he believes this to be a better use of his time. In the previous four years (the four years he could have spent in college) Fred has learned more than he ever thought possible in a relatively short period of time. It has now become his mission to educate and inspire others about what he has learned. Fred is an avid learner and reader, with an affinity towards teaching and personal growth. He hopes to help the world see as clearly as he has.

Connect with Fred on:

 Facebook: @frederickposimo

 Instagram: @fposimo

Or read Fred's blog, updated every Monday, Wednesday, & Friday at:

 Medium.com @frederickposimo

Here is a blank Goal Funnel for you to fill in your own goals:

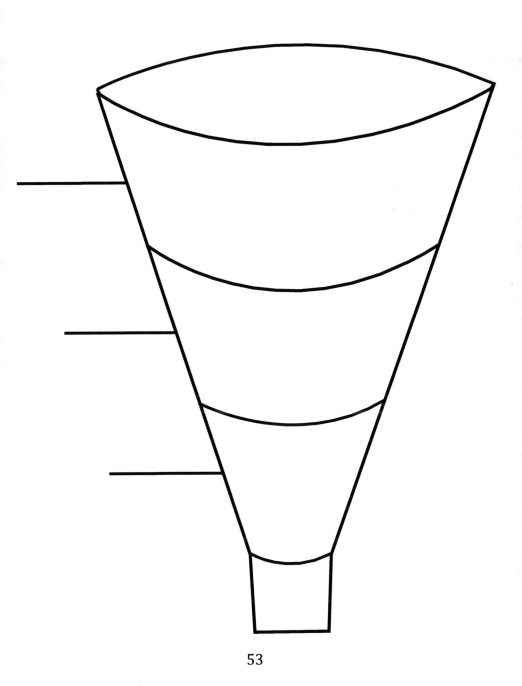